MW01251843

URBANITIES

URBANITIES

Brooke Clark

Fitzhenry & Whiteside

Text © 2020 Brooke Clark

All rights reserved. No part of this book may be reproduced in any manner without the express written consent of Fitzhenry & Whiteside, except in the case of brief excerpts in critical reviews and articles.

All inquiries should be addressed to

Fitzhenry & Whiteside.

Published in Canada by Fitzhenry & Whiteside

195 Allstate Parkway, Markham, ON   L3R 4T8

Published in the United States by

Fitzhenry & Whiteside

311 Washington Street, Brighton, MA   02135

Fitzhenry & Whiteside acknowledges with thanks the Canada Council for the Arts and the Ontario Arts Council for their support of our publishing program. We acknowledge the financial support of the Government of Canada through the Canada Book Fund (CBF) for our publishing activities.

Library and Archives Canada Cataloguing in Publication

Title: Urbanities / Brooke Clark.

Names: Clark, Brooke, 1972- author.

Description: Poems.

Identifiers: Canadiana 20200210807 | ISBN 9781554555369 (softcover)

Classification: LCC PS8605.L3615 U73 2020 | DDC C811/.6—dc23

Publisher Cataloging-in-Publication Data (U.S.)

Names: Clark, Brooke, author.

Title: Urbanities / Brooke Clark.

Description: Markham, Ontario : Fitzhenry & Whiteside, 2020. | Summary: "Sensuous, scandalous, satirical, tender, Brooke Clark's unique debut poetry collection is cynical and entertaining, replete with rich rhythms and playful rhymes" -- Provided by publisher.

Identifiers: ISBN 978-1-55455-536-9 (paperback)

Subjects: LCSH: Poetry. | BISAC: POETRY / General.

Classification: LCC PN6099.C637Ur | DDC 808.01 – dc23

Edited for press by Evan Jones

Design by Ken Geniza

Printed in Canada by Copywell

To Sharmila

Difficile est saturam non scribere.
—Juvenal

Contents

BOOK   II

Afterword

Acknowledgments

About the Author

Advertisement

You've picked it up and opened it, but just to have a look?
      Or should you take the time to read my book?
You're wondering if I can offer one compelling reason
      to pay good money for this slim collection,
so here's my pitch: I've tried to write some poems you might enjoy—
      a radical idea now, to deploy
the resources of poetry, not to stretch and strain
      syntax until it cracks, but to entertain.
And what if you don't like them? Fair enough—I'm not inclined
      to go through and explain them line by line,
or justify the choice of every word down to the letter.
      Maybe they're bad. Have you written something better?

(Martial)

BOOK   I

Scrambled Sonnet

Myron, if this world permitted me
to drift through leisured, empty days with you,
then I'd accept the opportunity
to dodge the minor sufferings we go through:
no buzz of the alarm, no subway press,
no cubicle's grey walls, no restlessness
in meeting rooms, no boredom-induced stress;
instead we would adopt the flaneur's ways,
talk as we walk, become habitués
of sunny public parks, bookstores, cafés—
but that is not our life. Necessity
binds us to jobs that we can't help but hate
for wasting our brief time so pointlessly.
Who, offered an escape, would hesitate?

(Martial)

A Wish

Chloe, your beauty makes me ache, yet you constantly refuse me.
  I wish you were less lovely—or less choosy.

(Martial)

Smallish Giant

Bruno's out drinking and holding forth on writing day and night,
  which only proves my point: he never writes.

(Lucian)

IMPORTANT: READ THIS FIRST

Don't read my poems before you've had a drink,
but careful—not too much before you start.
After a few, when you feel mildly drunk,
that's when you'll best appreciate my art.

(Martial)

To a Fortunate Feline

A sweet deal, Toast, being Chloe's pet:
you hop up on her lap and get
a giggle or a happy sigh;
your paw slides up her inner thigh,
demesnes denied the human hand...
I simply cannot understand:
for me, the moment's never right;
for you, perpetual green light.
She holds a finger for you to nip,
drops tender kisses on your lip,
then giggles as you lick her ear,
strokes your soft flank, seems pleased to hear
you purr; she makes an answering sound
and slides her heels along the ground,
her back curves and her eyes half-close
as if she were rapt in the throes
of ecstasy—then you both freeze,
pressed taut, as on an ancient frieze,
for several silent seconds—then
you both slip into calm again.
Worn out and ready for a nap
you stretch, yawning, across her lap
or, ignorant feline, coolly rest
your head against one heaving breast.
What can I say? I envy you.
I see her love is sometimes true.

(Catullus)

Perception and Reality

My poems aren't short enough, Bruno? There are worse ways to go wrong:
  your poems are short, it's true, but they feel long.

(Martial)

De gustibus ...

Chloe burns with love for Mitch, so none of us can have her.
  Mitch—with all the pallid charm of a cadaver.

(Martial)

Letter from an Unknown Writer

We met one night at a book launch,
      we drank, we talked, we laughed.
I said, "I'm writing a novel,"
      and you said, "Send me a draft."

So I sent it via email
      hoping a well-placed word
from you would get me started;
      I waited, but never heard.

Now you've published your latest
      and the critics applaud you in print,
it's a runaway bestseller
      and Hollywood's taken the hint.

I read it myself last weekend
      and my entrails turned to stone—
my book, but so badly rewritten
      you'd almost made it your own.

(Martial)

To a Bored Reader (Portrait of the Poet's Father)

You asked to read my poems, but now, a mere six pages in,
      I hear the sighs and stifled yawns begin.
I understand long epigrams don't interest everyone
      so this short one's for you. (That's it. You're done.)

(Martial)

On True Friendship

I don't mind open enemies, it's false friends I can't stand:
    the kind who gladly accept a helping hand,
say "Thanks" by stabbing you in the back, and then make cheap amends
    with "When I start a review, all friendship ends."

(Lucillius)

The Uncomfortable Truth of a Comfortable Hypocrite

"I'm a radical," says Brent, "my poems attack the establishment!"
    And yet he lives on grants from the government.

(Lucian)

Some Friend

Bruno stupidly introduced Mitch to his latest girlfriend;
    within an hour, Bruno was single again.

(Lucillius)

Economy

You're sick of my appeals, Lenore, and what's worse, you show it,
      but what options are there for a poet?
I'm living in a filthy, damp, unsanitary basement,
      and still I'm struggling to make the rent;
I sit alone here coughing every night, though I'd much rather
      be at readings, where the book crowd gathers,
but I don't have the entrance fee they charge you at the door,
      and then if I sneak in—I've tried before—
editors prefer the strivers who can buy them drinks.
      I can't afford paper and printer ink.
Even poetry journals have submission fees—they need
      some cash up-front before they'll deign to read
all the unagented crap that comes across the transom;
      my writing career is being held for ransom
and without some help from you, the truth is I can't pay.
      And still, knowing all that, you can say
I should cut back, and make my life more economical?
      What I live now is barely life at all.

(Martial)

Not Working

"Work in advertising," advises Laurence,
"there's money if you're good, and if you work."
But don't you see that's just the problem, Laurence?
Work for money? That's just—too much work.

(Martial)

Here, Let Me Help

Chloe, I pity you—you can't rouse Mitch's torpid lust,
        so here's a clue: on a shelf, collecting dust,
he keeps thousands of pages in a tilting, yellowing stack—
        drafts of the novel editors sent back
with nothing but a form rejection attached by paper clip.
        Your dad's in publishing—let that fact slip
next time you see Mitch kissing up to all the white-haired bores
        of literature. "My dad could…." Mitch is yours.

(Martial)

A Lucky Man

I envy Stan: although he has no talent for prose or verse,
      he's paid to teach a creative writing course.

(Aratus)

Frenemy

Bruno insults me behind my back? That's hardly a surprise.
      I'd be more offended by his praise.

(Apollinarius)

Silver Lining

You want whatever you say to be witty, Marcus,
      but your remarks are dense.
At least your wit—assuming it ever comes—
      has something to shine against.

(Martial)

The Amateur Tour

Ross, the shipping magnate's heir, shows little concern for us poor
     poets on this lengthy guided tour
through his home gallery of portraits, sculptures, photographs—
     "I thought my wife would kill me," he proudly laughs
pointing to a painting of a hanging, gutted deer;
     the price he paid would feed us for a year.
As he drones on we follow, smile, nod—how do we stand
     the never-ending boasting of a man
too vain to bother putting on false modesty's disguise?
     We know his fortune funds the Neptune Prize.

(Martial)

31

To a Hesitant Supporter

You say my writing's out of step with the readers of today;
      in a century (or two), I'll be read.
A pleasant fantasy, but will you help promote me now?
      Accolades are worthless to the dead.

(Anonymous)

Sweetness

Sweeter than the juice of a just-bitten apple on the tongue
        or the careless, uncouth laughter of the young,
sweeter than the sucrose-shock of suckled sugar cane
        or the scent of a garden after summer rain,
Chloe—that's how sweet the kisses you give Mitch seem to be;
        how much sweeter they'd taste if given to me.

(Martial)

The Girlfriend of a Friend

Browsing in a bookshop, we met by chance
one empty afternoon, and Bruno said
he'd take me by his latest girlfriend's place
so I could check her out and envy him;
her name was Emma—pretty and quick to laugh,
right off she struck me as much more my type.
Various topics led us here and there—
I couldn't help admiring her wit—
and then she asked me how I liked New York
and how much cash I made there—"Guys who do
a stint in New York always come back loaded."
I told the truth: nobody could get rich
in advertising today—marketing's
the first thing to get cut from every budget,
and anyway, I was writing poetry now.
I stopped; Emma looked disappointed, and,
propelled by a desire to shine for her
(and, yes, to wipe the smirk off Bruno's face)
I took a breath and (stupidly) went on,
"Of course things weren't so bad—I mean, I bought
the sweetest little Audi when I got back."
"A car!" she cried, delighted, "You have a car?"
A downtown, streetcar-riding type of girl,
to her a car shone as a luxury
that no one in her circle could provide.
Bruno's smirk withered as she grabbed my arm:
"Oh please," she sweetly cooed, "you have to let
me borrow it this weekend; I want to take
some friends out to the Prada warehouse sale
beyond the suburbs. Lend it to me—please?"

Naturally, there wasn't any car;
like her, I took the streetcar everywhere
snugly sardined amid the unwashed herd.
"I'm sure," said Bruno, "that he wouldn't mind—
would you?" His reborn smirk confronted me.
"What, me? Of course not, no … but … this weekend?
The thing is that, you see, I promised my,
uh, sister, that I'd drive her down to Kingston—
a friend of hers is getting married there,
and so, you see, I can't. I'm really sorry."
The door slammed shut behind us; Bruno asked,
"So, what did you think of her?" smiling at me.
"That bitch," I said, "dump her while you still can."

(Catullus)

False Dreams

Ross claims to envy poets their life of carefree penury,
    but lives amid the best things money can buy,
which he dismisses with a wave, then smooths his rumpled tux—
    no doubt he thinks God's words were, "Fiat luxe"—
and sighs, "Nobody gets how all this stuff oppresses me."
    To envy the poor is a rich man's luxury.

(Martial)

Epithalamium

Today Mitch finally marries Chloe; that was what it took
      to get her father to publish Mitch's book.
The fraudulence of the groom's love is the moment's only flaw;
      Mitch should swap vows with his father-in-law.

(Martial)

Pleasant Vacillation

Women and men have asked me to commit, but here's the truth:
some like one, some the other; I like both.

(Anonymous)

Something Missing

A charmless beauty can lure me in, but only for the night.
Beauty's just bait; charm is the hook inside.

(Capito)

Regifted

No doubt in a generous spirit, Lenore, and trying to give me a lift,
      you forwarded each thoughtful Christmas gift
that you received to me—amid the notebook, the Monet mug,
      the platter and the pseudo-Persian rug,
the brooch, the scarf, the jewellery box, the painted flower pot
      and the chocolates, I saw the vase I bought.
A mere dependant, I'm afraid of saying something rash,
      but since you care so much, next year—send cash.

(Martial)

Parfum

Marcus, you walk around wreathed in a pleasant aroma,
a mutedly masculine mixture of rawhide and spice,
yet I can't help but wonder what's under your perfume-shop aura;
any man who always smells nice doesn't really smell nice.

(Martial)

Contemporary Verse

Most poets suffer well-deserved neglect,
their intricately crafted lines all wrecked
by their own narcissism. Drawing on life,
they offer updates on their kids, their wife,
what birds they saw out on their morning walk,
the grackle's shrill song like the squeal of chalk
on blackboard—similes stuffed in the hearse
of that yielding, formless form, free verse.
Boxed in by the MFA shibboleth
that every turn of phrase has to be fresh
they twist their lines like Daedalus at his maze
or spew words into a pretentious haze
designed, not to reveal the striking essence
of some new thought, but to conceal thought's absence.
Their work's a half-developed Polaroid:
a depthless grey—a snapshot of the void.

(Philippus)

The Inferno

Bruno, you're always lending me books that appealed to you,
    and then you're hurt when I don't follow through.
Why won't I read what you suggest? I don't have time to waste
    and Hell, I've found, is other people's taste.

(Martial)

Math for Poets

"I read your book," says Bruno. "I thought half the poems were bad."
    If the other half were good, that's not half-bad.

(Martial)

Editor's Note

Some are good, some are bad, most mediocre at best.
That's how you fill a book, as any poet can attest.

(Martial)

Have Those Grapes Gone Sour?

People seem to enjoy my little epigrammatic flights
     though a certain poet has no appetite
(he claims) for stuff like that. Who cares? I'd much prefer my books
     appeal to readers—I don't cook for cooks.

(Martial)

Missing the Point

Whenever you sit down to write, you aim not to offend;
>you argue that it's art's role to defend
the voiceless, and create what you call a "discursive space"
>where absolutely everyone feels safe,
and judged against your goal not to offend, your work succeeds.
>No one's offended by what no one reads.

(Martial)

Rural Peace

I couldn't sleep in the city: every night
the streetlamps fired my window, halogen-bright,
car horns and people shouting filled my head
and buses seemed to drive right by my bed.
Each sound woke me like a shrill alarm,
but then Lenore lent me this little farm
among the fields and fences—and so now it's
still insomnia, but caused by crickets.

(Martial)

Surprise!

After all your support, I never expected this attack.
You pushed me forward, only to better stab me in the back.

(Martial)

Unexpected Wisdom

You write bad verse all day, but won't let anyone look at it.
      You're an idiot—and not an idiot.

(Martial)

The Hobby Farm

On certain summer days a breeze comes sweeping down
the hill onto this little hobby farm, and brings
        the sweet and piney scent of some
    unknown and distant stand of shady trees

that thoughtlessly perfume and cool the scorching air
and send it on its way. The moment they feel the breeze
        the neighbours raise their windows with
    relief, their children, newly energized,

run through the fields and chase the grasshoppers that fly
on paper-rustling wings among the waving blades
        of grass burnt brown that seem about
    to green again, as though in second spring.

You'd almost think that Pan, by blowing on his flute
had brought the breeze: the branches lighten, the leaves sing,
        even the stones shimmer with joy
    and the sky seems to press less heavily—

except, as we all know, the gods have left the earth
if they were ever here at all. But I will treat
        this breeze as though it were a god
    and worthy of thanks, and praise, and sacrifice:

whenever my nostrils catch the first of its cool scent
I nod in thanks and pour a sip's worth of my drink
        (a gin and tonic, usually)
    out on the ground to serve as a libation.

But no one joins me in these rites: an empty chair
sits next to mine, no second glass waits to be filled.
        I yearn to share my cool retreat;
     solitary pleasures sour the tongue.

And you, Jessica? Would a shade-stirred gin and tonic
delight your throat, parched by the city's blaze and fumes?
        Why crease your lovely brow with lines
     from squinting through the brutal glare that comes

in waves off cars and concrete cooked beneath the sun?
My broad trees offer shade from all hot irritations:
        Bruno's hot whispers, his hot stare,
     his hot hand on your neck and in your hair.

(Horace)

BOOK II

High Standards

I hate whatever novel everybody's praising now,
    I hate any café that draws a crowd,
I hate the kind of people who are friends with everyone—
    they're always "dropping by," always "have to run"—
I hate popularity and the gushing fans it brings.
    I prefer to seek out rarer things,
and beauty—beauty like yours—is vanishingly rare—but then,
    you've shared it with so many other men.

(Callimachus)

Promise Deferred

Your new book's full of impending death but Nestor, it's a lie.
    Live up to the promise of your poems: die.

(Martial)

Hot Tip

Here's my advice for how to shine on the epigram-writing scene:
    a poem should not mean, or be; it should be mean.

(Martial)

Inscribed on a Flyleaf

My book is out, and since I've got a few
spare author's copies, I'll send one to you.
I hope that I don't seem presumptuous
(you know how authors have to push themselves)
in wanting you to dedicate a spot
to it among the books that crowd your shelves.
But if you're struggling to find a place,
throw out Nestor's stuff—that'll clear some space.

(Martial)

A Misunderstanding

After years of failure—the unanswered queries, the silent phone—
    a small press editor says he loves your poems.
Are you finally poised to succeed? Have the scales really tipped?
    He wants you, Bruno, not your manuscript.

(Martial)

Unfulfilled Expectations

Inheriting his first wife's money was such a certainty
    Marcus picked out a villa in Tuscany
and had the renovations planned long before she was dead.
    At last she passed away. Her will was read
and he went back to basement apartments, diners and laundromats.
    She'd left it all to a home for ailing cats.

(Martial)

A Gentle Hint

Lenore, when the roof of this hobby farm, which nobody maintains,
    was leaking, and I swam in icy rains,
you sent a roofer with new shingles and, within a day,
    the farm could keep the strongest storm at bay.
Now the winds of December howl, and my old coat could be warmer:
    would you clothe the farm, but not the farmer?

(Martial)

The Way It Is

You gladly take work as a reviewer, Myron,
but then you savage every book you read.
You have to learn to moderate your opinion:
you can't be totally honest and succeed.

(Martial)

The Truth at Last

I lied in claiming to love your book. Our culture's wheels are greased
    with thousands of these small hypocrisies.

(Martial)

A Lucky Break

Nestor, you say a cough has left your broken voice no use.
    Don't read your poems then—we accept your excuse.

(Martial)

Left Out

Jessica called so I went over. I buzzed up—no reply.
      I'm sure she's up there with some other guy
while I'm stuck out here in the rain. Why don't I ever learn?
      And now what: go back home? Or wait my turn?

(Asclepiades)

An Atheist Turns to Prayer

Brevity comes easily, I've found, to anyone
    who wins a poetry prize; they say, "I won?
That's great!" They thank their editor and a few poet-friends
    who read an early draft, and that's the end.
Unlike the winner, the losers can't shut up: they've discovered
    the winner's best friend—or maybe her lover—
was on the judging panel, or claim they're being punished for
    a negative review from years before
in which they ripped off reputation's cloak, and left naked
    some now-forgotten poet then thought sacred,
proving they're independent of poetry's quid pro quo game
    and so for them, the end's always the same:
condemned by their integrity, they glumly stand aside
    and watch as their inferiors claim the prize.
But then, posterity ignores what's popular today,
    and who cares about prizes anyway?
I understand for those who lose complaining's a relief,
    but, god of prizes, let my words be brief.

(Callimachus)

To a Reader

Old books offer the order you seek
where every plot twist, no matter how bleak,
leads to the ending that always comes
with banns and gowns and chrysanthemums—
unlike what the moderns put you through:
they seem to suggest an image of you
curled by the lamp as approaching night
tightens its black noose around the light.

(Martial)

Highbrow Lowbrow

Advertising's been kind, so Laurence spent thousands on this soirée
    to launch his book—which he paid to publish himself.
But can he claw his way back up to the depths of poetry
    now that he has sunk to the heights of wealth?

(Palladas)

Not Again

The envelope, and—Nestor's won his seventh Neptune Prize.
        He stands, looks baffled, and his booze-blurred eyes
betray him: he heads for the exit rather than the stage.
        But some attendees, pitying his age,
seize and, with gentle hands, re-orient the drunken bard,
        steering him back to his unearned reward.
For fifty years he's been an icon, nationally respected
        for always staying true to the expected.
Tonight, fifty new pages of ruminative free-verse dreck
        capture a fifty-thousand dollar cheque
and add another accolade to his grand legacy
        of unwearying mediocrity.
A mid-speech fit of coughing leaves him bent, gasping for breath.
        His career lacks one accomplishment: his death.

(Bassus of Smyrna)

Quid Pro No

In reviewing your book last spring, I called it a masterpiece.
        Of course, I had one eye on the release
of my own book that fall, thinking you'd puff me in return.
        You didn't, and now you act shocked to learn
that I'll be trashing your new book? You broke a sacred code
        by withholding the false praise I was owed.

(Martial)

You're Welcome

You crashed with me for the weekend, Bruno, and, in desperation,
  scanned my old notebooks in search of inspiration.
Now what you stole, published as yours, makes critics fawn and dote.
  My cast-offs are the best things you never wrote.

(Martial)

Another Failure

My reasons for dumping Jessica were laid out in my mind.
        She came by with a bottle—I thought the wine
would give me courage for a final, permanent goodbye;
        I drank, but then just stared into her eyes
as she leaned close and dropped her shoulder to let one dress-strap fall—
        I couldn't fight both love and alcohol.

(Rufinus)

Nice Try

You say you'll read through my new poems and offer some suggestions?
    I think you're scouting for your next collection.

(Martial)

Don't Ask Me How I Know

Nestor, those young poets who take you out and drink your health
    are only wishing for one thing: your death.

(Martial)

Unpleasantries

A stranger eyed me up and then approached
as I was sitting in a small café
and said, "Aren't you—aren't you the guy who writes
those funny little poems?" I didn't say
a word, but gave a nod, and tried to act
as though this happened to me every day,
but then he followed with, "You look so ... threadbare."
I stiffened slightly: "Funny poems don't pay."
"Guess not," he said, and with a little grin
that turned into a smirk, he walked away.
The fate of unacknowledged legislators:
careless mockery from passing strangers.

(Martial)

Advice Not Taken

You've often given me the same unsolicited advice:
    "Forget these little things, write a big book."
Instead of that advice, I wish that you could give me time,
    the time a university can give
to its professor-poets, Myron, the long-drawn afternoons
    in offices where dead ideas await
their exhumation, where no student's hesitating step
    vexes the silence of the sepulchre.
The book I'd write would earn me every newspaper critic's praise
    and pluck me—briefly—from among the shades.

(Martial)

Evidence

Don't bother, Jessica: your hair's all tangled, you reek
     of last night's wine and weed, your left cheek
is raw with whisker burns, where your neck curves out to meet
     your shoulder I see purpled prints of teeth,
and now your phone starts buzzing. You reach for it—I feel like Zeus:
     new gods have rendered me superfluous.

(Meleager)

Inevitable

I drank and smoked, stayed out all night, I hopped from bed to bed—
    who claims they haven't?—but now, on my head,
silver strands flash amid the black, and in several spots
    my scalp gleams through. Time for serious thoughts.

(Philodemus)

Why Not?

Live to please yourself. You might as well—everyone else
will criticize regardless, some more, some less.

(Mimnermus)

To J— M—

We won't admit that you are gone, when there are countless ways
the good you did in life outlives your days.

(Callimachus)

Mentem mortalia tangunt

I'd resolved to write a masterpiece that would win me instant fame
     and make the ages echo with my name,
but, passing a graveyard, I recalled that all lives share one end.
     I might as well go drinking with my friends.

(Anonymous)

Numen

That man seems like a god to me—he seems
more than a god, sitting there beside you
and leaning close so he can hear you speak.
He whispers in your ear

and when your laughter starts, stretches an arm
around your shoulders, calmly pulls you close—
my voice dies in my throat, my heavy tongue
lolls witless in my mouth,

a slender stream of lava rushes through
my veins, a roaring deafens both my ears,
my eyes go dark, as though someone has flicked
the world around me off.

My soft life has destroyed me. I watch the days
slip past, too weak to seize the things I want.
I perish like an ancient princeling, sunk
in worthless luxuries.

(Catullus)

Parenting Tip

Whether you use discipline or act like you're their friend,
     your kids will learn to hate you in the end.

(Mimnermus)

Message to the Young

Death begins at conception, and what we call being alive
     is really just the time it takes to die.

(Anonymous)

Still Waiting

You say your memoirs offer pointed re-evaluations
    of countless authors' puffed-up reputations
so you've arranged to have them published once you're safely dead.
    Nestor, it's time your memoirs were read.

(Martial)

On the Happy Life

Here are a few things, Myron, I have learned:
happiness lies in wealth bequeathed, not earned,
in mansions, cars, expensive clothes, fine wine,
and being blessed with the priceless sort of mind
that never expects daily reality
to match the ideals of philosophy.
Lacking those things, you'll have to turn to drink
to quell despair, the curse of those who think,
or try pot, hash, coke, crack or crystal meth,
wish you were someone else, and wait for death.

(Martial)

An Untimely Death

Stuck in a financial district traffic jam, a man—
    mid-forties, with a wife and kids at home—
was killed when a nearby building dropped a giant icicle
    that pierced his car's steel roof and then his skull.
Death came too suddenly for him to even make a sound;
    the fragile blade had melted in the wound
before the ambulance arrived. The paramedics paused
    at death inflicted by a vanished cause.

(Martial)

An Emerging Diogenes

One of the cardinal rules of life, expressed by a budding cynic:
    the poor go to jail, the rich to the rehab clinic.

(Lucillius)

Against Sobriety

The dead are sober. Pour—I want to drink my thoughts away.
    Already, age has flecked my hair with grey.

(Apollonides)

Holiday

Everywhere snowbanks have melted, the stream flows loud with the run-off;
    nevertheless, on the hill
under the parking lot's edge, a few last drifts, memories of winter
    dirty with time, have survived.
Now is the yellow-and-brown spring, green still only a promise
    hovering over the boughs,
the sharp-edged breeze able to suddenly cut the sun's warmth
    out of the clear, bright air.
Fishermen stand in the shallows and roll-cast lures at the deep runs
    haunted by tremulous fish;
sometimes a rod bends double, a man stoops, raises a slim form
    sculpted from shimmering light.
Women rehearsing for summer, their sunglasses rescued from drawers,
    stride along still-damp paths,
warm enough wearing just leggings with short-sleeved T-shirts or hoodies,
    walking their children or dogs.
Thick fist clutching his lame cane, one bent grandfather shuffles
    after a scampering girl
who, all giggles and blown curls, urges him, "Can't you go faster?"
    racing away down the path.
Spring merely ushers in summer, whose bright green beauties the orange-red
    autumn consumes in its turn;
too soon winter returns with its chill, and lowers a pale shroud
    over the comatose earth.

We are not meant for eternity, nor should we look with fresh hope
        up to the ignorant sky:
though we have watched as the swift moon dies by degrees, then is reborn
        gradually out of the dark,
we can't regain lost time, or escape from the burden of long years;
        when death seeks us out
love, friends, family, all the achievements of life, will be nothing;
        then we are shadows and dust.

(Horace)

Finally

I went online this morning and nearly laughed at what I found:
    Nestor is finally headed underground.
Heart failure, caused by alcohol, caught up with him at home;
    his body sprawled on one last worthless poem
demonstrated that he scribbled right to the very brink
    of death—his last breath dried his last line's ink.
He was the cynosure of our time's ersatz poetry
    so let's ask one prayer of posterity:
may black mould overspread his books and worms devour their pages
    to keep them from the eyes of future ages.

(Martial)

A Request

Mark, I want to ask you for a favour:
could you get Jerome to write about
my book of poems? I gave you a copy
almost two months ago, when it came out.
I ask because you both work at the paper
and you can read the tide-shifts of his mood,
and so one day—I leave it up to you
to pick a moment when he has subdued
his violence with a column savaging
some poor young writer who has no defence
and, gorged with the lifeblood of a young career,
he has a moment of benevolence
and starts to feel that urge he sometimes gets
to seem a champion of literature
by praising some new author no one knows—
yes, I realize those moods are rare,
but try, please, for my little book—its spine
not even cracked, its pages not yet curled
by readers' hands—it needs some powerful
reviewer to help launch it in the world.
If I can't get myself in the Books section
no publisher will take my next collection.

(Martial)

At a Child's Funeral

Today we give to the earth the body of our little girl,
      our little darling; we'll never watch her twirl
around the house again in her impenetrable games
      or listen as she wheedles and whines our names
in that annoying tone we tried to break her of before;
      now we'd give anything to hear it once more.
She'll find whatever waits for all of us when this life ends—
      eternal silence or the souls of friends—
while, left behind, we bow our heads to see what prayers can do.
      Lie lightly, earth—she stepped so lightly on you.

(Martial)

It's Better to Burn Out

But youth, our time of strength and beauty, pinnacle of life,
      is like the blossoms of the spring—too brief;
pursuing love and joy, we never notice that beneath
      the sun we cast two shadows: age and death,
and of these, age is worst—though old, you'll still be scorched by lust,
      but everyone rejects you with disgust.
The truth is, once your prime has passed—after, say, forty-five—
      you're probably better off dead than alive;
there's nothing more waiting for you but slow-dragging time
      as you sink through the stages of decline:
at first mere aches and pains, and then fatigue, forgetfulness,
      the stumbling from one illness to the next,
watching with something close to envy as your stricken friends
      accept with gratitude their early ends,
burying, perhaps, your child, your husband or your wife,
      hating the lingering disease of life.
It's better to die early than suffer the pain of going on;
      true happiness is given to no one.

(Mimnermus)

Envoi

So that's my book. Such trifles don't make a literary star,
      but they can't have been all bad—you read this far.
Stardom's for those whose luminous lines sear with sincerity.
      You laughed a few times? Good enough for me.

(Martial)

Dedication

It used to be no author could afford
to publish till he'd praised some in-bred lord
in a fulsome dedicatory epistle
(which most readers would have given a miss, I'll
bet)—but now such flattery's grown rare
since literary power's moved elsewhere.
So, little book, I dedicate you to
the influential book reviewers, who
will pass you on, immortal, to the ages
through their evanescent newsprint pages.
Lacking such support, you won't be able
to dodge the shame of the remainder table
where once-new books lie like neglected lovers
gathering dust on their unopened covers.
To the critics, then—through them, you'll outwit time
and not require such poor protection as mine.

(Martial)

Afterword

I first fell in love with the Latin poet Marcus Valerius Martialis (Martial) through a textbook. A few of his simpler, two-line epigrams were the first genuine Latin literature that I could appreciate, and these caustic poems practically jumped off of pages otherwise devoted to explanations of the subjunctive mood or the ablative absolute.

The original impetus behind this book was to try to capture some of what I loved about Martial in English. Along the way I added poems by Catullus and Horace, and then some from the Greek Anthology and the Greek lyric poets. (The authors whose epigrams I've adapted are identified in brackets after each poem.) These are not direct translations, however, and none of the poems in this book is a particularly good guide to what the original actually says. Instead, I took the approach that in the eighteenth century was called "imitation": to rewrite the poem as the author would have written it were he alive and writing today. Where the poems refer to ancient customs or social life, I have tried to come up with contemporary equivalents, so that a reader can understand the poem directly, as its original readers would have, without the mediation of scholarly notes. And while I have not attempted to copy classical metres in English (with one exception), I have used rhyme and metre to capture some of the formal qualities that make the Greek and Latin originals poetry.

The willingness to be shocking, to push at the margins of good taste and give voice to thoughts that are generally repressed, is one of the characteristics of the epigram. Think of it as a rude, disreputable uncle who shows up at poetry's genteel garden party and tells dirty jokes. And perhaps poetry could stand to be a little more like the wolf in La Fontaine's fable: unwilling to be domesticated by polite society, despite the comfort and material advantages it offers.

Acknowledgments

Some of these poems originally appeared, sometimes in different form, in the following journals: *Able Muse, Arion, Light, Lighten Up Online, The Literateur, Literary Imagination, Partisan, The Rotary Dial, Snakeskin*, and *The Tangerine*. My thanks to the editors and staff.

I owe a tremendous debt of gratitude to Mark Young, who tutored me from the first chapter of *Wheelock's Latin* all the way to Virgil's *Aeneid*; to Myron McShane, who unravelled the complexities of ancient metre; and to Craig Proctor and Matt Tierney, who offered early encouragement.

I want to thank Evan Jones for his thoughtful and sensitive editing and his belief in the manuscript, and everyone at Fitzhenry & Whiteside for making this book a reality.

About the Author

Brooke Clark studied English literature at the University of Toronto and Queen's University. His poetry, essays and reviews have appeared in journals in Canada, the U.S. and the U.K., including *The Walrus, Arion* and *Literary Imagination.*

He lives in Toronto. This is his first book.